'Moral Injury Towards a Theology' is fantastic! It is easy to read and very logical. It explains nitty gritty doctrine and shows why it is necessary for effectual life application. The style is very similar to Martyn Lloyd-Jones in that respect. Also, the personal testimony is very impactful. I hope many people read it and are blessed by it as I have been. **Peter Humphreys**, PhD candidate.

To anyone thinking about this book, it is well written and based on Neil's wealth of practical experience as an army chaplain. It is invaluable in understanding why you may feel the way you do after witnessing trauma. **Troy Hartley**, Firefighter

MORAL INJURY
Towards a Theology

NEIL CULLAN McKINLAY

Published by WEEMAC Publishing©

March 2025

Cover design by my big brothers and my niece. So grateful to Fearghas MacFhionnlaigh, Stuart McKinlay and Cara Mairi Bell.

CONTENTS

Introduction

As an ordained Presbyterian minister, I qualified to become an Army Chaplain in early 2008. At that time, I began work as a Reservist (part time) and started working fulltime in early 2013. Immediately I began rubbing shoulders with individuals suffering from 'problems', some of which are now being labelled as Moral Injury. I got to interact with doctors, Mental Health nurses and various psychologists. What could a Presbyterian Minister such as myself have to say about mental health issues? Says Sarah Gibson,

> Moral injury is not just a 'mental health' issue because it relates to much more than the mind. Moral injury is also a state of the heart and a condition of the spirit. As a chaplain I know something about these things and believe my chaplain colleagues have something worthwhile to contribute as we discharge our overarching duty of care.[1]

Moral Injury pertains to having one's view of the world violated resulting in an adverse effect of feeling guilt and shame. A worldview is that aspect of our humanity that focuses on things in the world that are (in our own personal opinion) right or wrong, and true or false. Thus, morals relate to who we are as a person. Therefore, morals are the personal apparatus

---

[1] Sarah Gibson, *Moral Injury: Unseen Wounds in an Age of Barbarism*, (Edited by Tom Frame), University of New South Wales Press Ltd, 2015, 234.

which we use as individuals to determine, judge or deem what measures up or fails to measure up to our own set of moral standards.

Moral standards vary from individual to individual. In other words, some individuals have a high moral standard, and some have a low moral standard. But who gets to judge whether a moral standard is high or low? Upon what does one base one's morals? The tendency might be to posit "Common Sense" as the answer. However, this approach is to take too much for granted.

Morals are rules. They are a set of laws by which we police the world in which we live. They govern our interactions with others and our behaviour towards them and they determine how we perceive the interactions between others, whether as individuals or in groups.

Moral Injury occurs when as individuals we go against our own set of moral values and cause harm. It is important to note that this harm may or may not involve other parties (whether human, animal, objects or anything else). The bottom line is that Moral Injury is an injury to self! It's a form of self-harm so to speak. And, because morals vary from individual to individual it would be wrong to say that morals are simply the application of "Common Sense" to life issues. Says Tom Frame,

> The term moral injury gained currency from the late 2000s among researchers in the United

States who believed that something distinct, and perhaps new, was adversely affecting American service personnel returning from combat operations… Sufferers of moral injury struggle to discern good and bad, right and wrong in personal morality and social conventions after being somewhere when the norms of civilised society were collapsing, or after engaging with a people displaying little or no regard for basic human rights and entitlements… The health of a person's soul and state of their moral being are not the privileged possessions of behavioural scientists.[2]

Moral Injury is self-inflicted! It is caused when you as an individual do not measure up to or have violated your own code of ethics and your conscience accuses you with regular reminders (usually in the wee small hours of the night) resulting in you experiencing feelings of guilt and shame.

> Guilt is one of the most powerfully paralysing forces to the human spirit.[3]

Human beings demonstrably are moral agents. But where do our morals come from? From our parents? Our community? Thin air? If morals are really just applied "Common Sense" then why, no matter how

---

[2] Tom Frame, *Moral Injury: Unseen Wounds in an Age of Barbarism*, (Edited by Tom Frame), University of New South Wales Press Ltd, 2015, 2.
[3] RC Sproul, Guilt and Guilt Feelings by R.C. Sproul from Guilt and Forgiveness (ligonier.org)

low they are, do none of us ever live up to our own moral standards? And why then do we judge the conduct of others to be wanting at times?

In the following we shall argue that morals are spiritual. By spiritual we mean that morals reside in the innermost being of humans, i.e., the conscience so-called, and as such, morals are invisible to the naked eye. The individual's conscience is injured when the conscience refuses to excuse his/her thoughts and/or words and/or deeds.

Our actions (whether thought/word/deed) have consequences, moral consequences, i.e., *spiritual* consequences. Thus, Moral Injury is a spiritual problem.

Sarah Gibson underlines the need for theological input into the Moral Injury question,

> I can readily understand why a healthcare professional can look at a religious practitioner or spiritual counsellor and wonder who they are encountering and what the patient or client might be getting from them. But I also note that healthcare professionals are not generally educated in the nuances of existential thought, they are not trained to deal with spiritual questions and moral dilemmas. They will have their own opinions, of course. But they have not been required to immerse themselves in the history of ideas, to become familiar with philosophy's response to enduring questions of

identity and destiny, to recognise and respond to the heart's yearnings for point and purpose in life. These are existential matters in which healthcare professionals cannot generally claim any expertise.[4]

Theology[5] is the study of God as He has revealed Himself in His creation and in His written Word. The Bible teaches us about God, His creation and ourselves as human beings. It teaches us about what is wrong with us and what God has done, is doing and will do about our problem. Therefore, *Moral Injury: Towards a Theology* will help us to understand why Moral Injury exists and how it can be cured in terms of the Bible.

---

[4] Sarah Gibson, *Moral Injury: Unseen Wounds in an Age of Barbarism*, (Edited by Tom Frame), University of New South Wales Press Ltd, 2015, 230.
[5] The author writes from a Biblically Reformed theological perspective commonly known as "Covenant Theology."

Man: God's Moral Agent

When Gentiles, who do not have the law, by nature do the things in the law, these, although not having the law, are a law to themselves, who show the work of the law written in their hearts, their conscience also bearing witness, and between themselves *their* thoughts accusing or else excusing *them.*
Romans 2:14-15

Introduction

In order to understand what morals have to do with us as individuals, each of us having a conscience, we will need to delve into what the Bible, i.e., God's revelation to us, has to say. Therefore, we shall begin with a little history:

At the time of Moses (circa 1500BC) God gave the Hebrews a set of instructions called God's Law. Ordinarily, God's Law refers to the Ten Commandments or Decalogue. This is God's Moral Law. However, from the time of Moses to the time of Christ the body of God's Law also included civil or judicial and ceremonial applications.

Ceremonial Law

Ceremonial Law included the sacrificial system which revolved around the Tabernacle and subsequently the Temple at Jerusalem. This period of administration was fulfilled when that which it typified appeared. Jesus Christ is THE Lamb of God who takes away the sin of the world. The *Ceremonial*

Law, therefore, was the Gospel or the Good News of and about Jesus Christ administered in picture form, and as such, the Saviour and what He was coming to do was displayed to the Hebrews throughout Old Testament times.

The Ceremonial Law with its symbols and symbolic depictions is no longer needed now that that which it depicted has come. The sacrifice of bulls, doves, goats and lambs, the sprinkling of their blood on people and objects, the pouring of blood on the Seat of Atonement on the Ark of the Covenant in the Holy of Holies by the High Priest dressed in linen wearing an ephod have all served their intended purpose, as have the Temple building and even Jerusalem, the City of David itself. All pointed to the Great High Priest and what He was coming to do. Jesus Christ is the Great High Priest who offered up Himself to take away (i.e., to cover over, blot out) the sins of His people. As John the Baptiser said of Jesus when He saw Him walking towards him to be baptised by him, "Behold! The Lamb of God who takes away the sin of the world!" John 1:29b.

The Ceremonial Law's connection to the Moral Law (i.e., the Ten Commandments or Decalogue) was that it illustrated or pictured what needed to be done to atone for sin, i.e., for the individual's (and the nation's) breaking of the Moral Law in thought, word and deed. "And according to the law almost all things are purified with blood, and without the shedding of blood there is no remission" Hebrews 9:22. (*cf.* Leviticus 17:11.)

Judicial or Civil Law

Judicial or *Civil Law* was simply the application of the Moral Law (i.e., the Ten Commandments) on a national level, covering such things as how, when, and where God was to be worshiped and how the Hebrews were to interact with each other.

The *Judicial* or *Civil Law* was no longer needed when Israel was dissolved as a nation after Christ's death and resurrection, but more particularly when the Temple, as predicted by Jesus, was destroyed in 70 AD. The Hebrew people were commanded to take the Gospel into all the world, i.e., into every other nation.

Soon Gentiles (the *ethnoi* or Ethnics) began to be engrafted into the same vine as believing Hebrews as the Gospel began to spread throughout the world beginning from Jerusalem. Thus, Israel was no longer a nation with national borders, but became that ever-expanding spiritual entity called the Church. The Church is the outward (and albeit imperfect) expression on earth of the perfect Kingdom of Heaven. However, whether Jew or Gentile, both are one under the headship of Christ Jesus. That which remains of ancient Israel's *Judicial* or *Civil Law* is its general equity or principles.

The Moral Law

The *Moral Law* is that which is summarised in the Ten Commandments and is summarised again in the command to love God and your neighbour as yourself. The Moral Law is an outward expression of the character of the triune God. The Father loves the Son and the Spirit. The Son loves the Father and the Spirit. The Spirit loves the Father and the Son. Each Person in the Godhead loves God. Thus, God from all eternity loves God and His neighbour as Himself.

The Image of God

Only Man is made in the image and likeness of God. Thus, Man has been designed and engineered by God to love God and his neighbour as himself. It is when the individual fails to do this that the individual experiences pangs of conscience. The Apostle Paul under inspiration of the Holy Spirit says, "When Gentiles, who do not have the law, by nature do the things in the law, these, although not having the law, are a law to themselves" Romans 2:14. In other words, God's Law previously had been given only to the Hebrews. However, even though the Gentiles do not have God's Law, they are still able by nature, i.e., naturally, to do things taught in God's Law – things like looking after the elderly, the sick and the infirm. They may honour parents and condemn adultery, stealing and lying. Thus, they that do not have the (written) Law, as Paul goes on to say, "show the work of the law written in their hearts." Therefore, God's Moral Law, (which reveals God's character), is written on the heart of every human being.

The Conscience

The Apostle goes on to say how the Moral Law operates in the heart of the individual, i.e., "their conscience also bearing witness, and between themselves *their* thoughts accusing or else excusing *them.*" Our conscience judges our thoughts, words, and actions. If we do not meet the moral standard, our conscience accuses us. Thus, our conscience is like a little policeman we carry around in our head, who either accuses or excuses us when we involve ourselves in moral decisions and actions.

Summary

In summary, the Moral Law given by God through Moses to the ancient Hebrews on tablets of stone is the same Moral Law that is written on the heart of every human being. Our conscience accuses us, not because there is something wrong with God's Law, rather because there is something wrong with each one of us. The Apostle says that, "we suppress the truth in unrighteousness" Romans 1:18b. This is to say that because we are fallen we try to keep an internal lid on what may be known of God, (i.e., His character as expressed in His Moral Law as it is written in our hearts and witnessed to by the external written Ten Commandments). That great Reformer of the Church put it like this,

> It is a fact that the law of God which we call the moral law is nothing else than a testimony of natural law and of that conscience which God has engraved upon the minds of men.[6]

The Two Ways God Reveals Himself

There are two ways in which God reveals Himself to fallen humanity. The first is twofold: The things He has made which includes our conscience. And the

---

[6] John Calvin, *Institutes of the Christian Religion*, IV, xx, 16.

second is the Scriptures. However, since we are fallen creatures, the former cannot properly be understood without the latter. Thus, the Ten Commandments, which are written on stone, confirm that which is written on the heart. In other words, the subjective can be confirmed only by the objective. However, in order to effectively silence an accusing conscience, one first has to be reconciled to the Author of the Moral Law!

Military Context

For decades and perhaps centuries those involved in military conflict have encountered people displaying what used to be known as "Shell Shock", then "Battle Fatigue" and now "Post-Traumatic Stress Disorder" (PTSD). PTSD has been defined as,

> A fear – victim reaction to a perceived life threat. It has clinical symptoms of flashbacks, nightmares, hyper-vigilance, dissociation. Then, in America in December 2009, a slightly different (but perhaps related) disorder began to be discussed. It was referred to by psychologists as "Moral Injury."[7]

It has been stated that, "Moral Injury is an inner conflict based on moral self assessment of having inflicted or failed to prevent significant harm. Its symptoms are excessive guilt, loss of meaning, anger and shame."

---

[7] See for example,
http://www.sciencedirect.com/science/article/pii/S02727358090 00920

As 'moral injury' is more an existential and spiritual crisis than a psychological dysfunction, psychologists have pointed out the limited therapeutic impact that standard cognitive interventions can offer. The suggestion that effective assistance for moral injury involves some sort of confession and forgiveness within a moral framework has moved the discussion into territory usually covered by chaplains. The implicit faith-based and moral set of assumptions which under-gird pastoral transactions in chaplaincy are precisely what appears to be needed in repairing moral injury.[8]

Summary

Like all moral dilemmas "Moral Injury" is a problem of the conscience. Oswald Chambers got it right when he said, "Conscience is the internal perception of God's Moral Law." Therefore, anyone with a conscience is aware of God's Law. The Apostle Paul says, "The Law was our tutor to bring us to Christ, that we might be justified by faith" Galatians 3:24. Thus, the accusing conscience, by revealing God's Moral Law on our heart, demonstrates to the individual their need for Christ, the Saviour of sinners. Therefore, the inner conflict of conscience can be remedied by Jesus Christ revealed only in the Gospel.

---

[8] Tim Dyer of John Mark Ministries
http://www.defenceanglicans.org.au/moral-injury-and-moral-repair-the-emerging-discussion-within-the-armed-forces/

Man: Triune in Nature

Now may the God of peace Himself sanctify you completely; and may your whole spirit, soul, and body be preserved blameless at the coming of our Lord Jesus Christ. 1 Thessalonians 5:23

Introduction

In the following we will discuss in broad terms the makeup of the individual human being living in the world today. The Bible reveals God as Triune, i.e., Father and Son and Holy Spirit. When God said, "Let Us make man in Our own image" He really meant it. Being Triune, God is the original One and Many, the General and the Particular, Unity in Diversity paradigm. The Father is not the Son or the Spirit. The Son is not the Father or the Spirit. The Spirit is not the Father or the Son. Yet the three are one God. However, keep in mind that God is not made up of three parts. Rather each of the three persons interpenetrates the others. Man, the image and likeness of God, has three interpenetrating aspects: spirit and soul and body.

Military Healthcare

Whether consciously or not the Military cares for each of the three interconnected aspects of man. In general terms the Chaplain ministers to the *spirit*, the psychologist/psychiatrist attends to the *soul* (or *mind*), and the doctor works on the *body*. Working towards the healing of the individual works best when the Chaplain and the Psychologist/Psychiatrist and the Doctor compare notes on the individual member's progress. A broken leg, for example, can have a diverse effect on the spirit and the soul!

The Chaplain, the Psych and the Doctor
The Doctor perhaps has the easier task of the three in helping to mend a broken soldier. Again, in general terms, unlike the Chaplain and the Psych, the Doctor works with the visible. In an effort to simplify things, let us say for argument's sake that a broken leg, e.g., is attended to more easily than a broken spirit or a troubled soul/mind. The latter two ailments manifest themselves only through the member's behaviour and his/her verbal communications.

It is far easier to mask or hide a mental or a spiritual problem than a damaged or broken limb! In the Military context a member may be afraid to reveal mental health problems on account of a real or perceived fear that it may lead to an early discharge or adversely affect the possibility of a future promotion. Thus, some members' mental problems may remain undetected for an extended and unhealthy period without available treatment. This is why it is imperative that the trinity of Chaplain, Psych and Doctor regularly compare with each other (what they can) about an individual's state of wellbeing.

Moral Injury
Since "Moral Injury" (MI) is a spiritual problem, it comes under the domain of the Chaplain's area of expertise. MI is a problem of the conscience. The conscience is the moral centre or moral compass of a human being. The Chaplain can work to help the

member silence or at least mitigate an accusing conscience by helping the member be reconciled to God through His Mediator, i.e., Jesus Christ.

God's forgiveness translates into self-forgiveness. Whenever the member is ready to forgive him/herself then the Moral Injury is ready to be healed. Healing comes through trusting in God that He really has forgiven you on account of what Jesus Christ did on the cross. The Holy Spirit (working with God's Word) does the actual convincing. Thus, the Triune God, Father, Son, and Holy Spirit, work together (through the instrument of the Chaplain) to heal the member.

PTSD

Immediately it can be seen that the Chaplain, because he is dealing with a tortured conscience, is encroaching on the area of expertise delegated to the Psych. The conscience is an aspect of the soul or mind. This is to be expected on account of the makeup of a human being being spirit and soul and body. A useful description of the individual human being is that he/she is a soul-spirit with a body.

Post-Traumatic Stress Disorder (PTSD) has been defined as, "A sub-conscious reactive dysfunction where the normal fear suppression processes that get linked and integrated into coherent memory are not in place." Thus, there is turmoil in the member's innermost being (the soul or mind). Certain aspects of the soul or mind are out of sync with each other. The member experiences emotions connected with fear and is unable consciously to control them because of a disconnect with the normal process of memory.

We do not want to trivialise the emotions experienced by the sufferer of PTSD but, by way of simplistic example, most of us have experienced some panic when we cannot remember the exact spot where we parked our car or if we turned off the stove before we left for work. Did we lock the house when we left? We rack our brains trying to remember. We go through the process of remembering step by step while keeping the whole thing in perspective – "It's only a car…", "We have house insurance…" etc. However, the PTSD sufferer may have unexpected panic and anxiety attacks with no means of controlling them which in turn ratchets-up the episode and the sufferer may lose all sense of perspective.

Physical Ailment
Tom Frame reminds us that there are distinct and at times identifiable differences between Moral Injury and PTSD,

> A person can have sustained moral injury and PTSD and there will be some with moral injury and no symptoms of PTSD. They are not synonymous.[9]

---

[9] Tom Frame, *Moral Injury: Unseen Wounds in an Age of Barbarism*, (Edited by Tom Frame), University of New South Wales Press Ltd, 2015, 254.

However, Rhiannon Neilsen reminds us that it is sometimes difficult to differentiate the two where she says,

> Although there is no universally agreed definition, moral injury is generally understood as the 'negative outcomes following a transgression of deeply held moral values and beliefs'.
> The field of psychology has dominated investigations aimed at determining whether moral injury can be understood as an experience distinct from existing conditions, such as PTSD, by looking at differences in the symptoms and the emotional response. While this method is useful for prognosis, it leaves much unsaid and unaccounted for. Indeed, there is significant overlap between the symptoms of PTSD and moral injury.[10]

Moral Injury and PTSD may at times have a detrimental effect on the member's physical health. Again, this is because the spirit and the soul and the body are one integrated whole. As mental exercises and stimulation are to PTSD's coping strategies, so diet and exercise are important components of physical wellbeing. A healthy body will more readily cope with and heal a physical ailment. However, at first blush it would seem that a healthy body may not assist in mitigating any of the pain of those suffering

---

[10] Rhiannon Neilsen, *Moral Injury: Unseen Wounds in an Age of Barbarism*, (Edited by Tom Frame), University of New South Wales Press Ltd, 2015, 136.

from the symptoms of PTSD and/or Moral Injury. However, if we keep in mind that the spirit and the soul and the body interpenetrate each other, we must conclude that there must be some, albeit perhaps small, benefit to maintaining, as far as the member is able, physical fitness. The old adage "Healthy body, healthy mind" does have something going for it.

Summary

Human beings are triune by nature. They are not three parts, because God, in whose image they are made, is not three parts. Rather as each aspect of the Godhead (Father and Son and Holy Spirit) interpenetrates the Others, so the human being's body and soul and spirit interpenetrate each other. Thus, total healing is healing of the body and the soul and the spirit.

Conclusion

Moral Injury is to have your own conscience accuse you and blame you for some action you did or failed to do. Notice what the Apostle Paul says,

> Now may the God of peace Himself sanctify you completely; and may your whole **spirit**, **soul**, and **body** be preserved blameless at the coming of our Lord Jesus Christ. 1 Thessalonians 5:23.

God will completely sanctify those who have been reconciled to Him by and through Jesus Christ. This means that God will work in you to repair you – body and soul and spirit! He will wholly transform you. He will preserve you "blameless," which is to say that

God will hold you blameless on Judgment Day on account of what Jesus has done *for* you and the Holy Spirit has done *in* you.

Our healing comes through faith alone. If we believe that God has forgiven us our sins, then we must stop blaming ourselves for them! Moral Injury is cured by trusting that God has forgiven you, which in turn causes you to behave as if you really believe this good news!

Man: Fallen in Nature

"Therefore, just as through one man sin entered the world, and death through sin, and thus death spread to all men, because all sinned ... as through one man's offence *judgment* came to all men, resulting in condemnation, even so through one Man's righteous act *the free gift* came to all men, resulting in justification of life. For as by one man's disobedience many were made sinners, so also by one Man's obedience many were made righteous." Romans 5:12 & 18-19

Introduction

As the above verses attest, the Bible teaches that the first man, Adam, federally represented mankind before God. After God had created Adam (and the rest of His creation) Scripture says, "Then God saw everything He had made, and indeed it was very good" Genesis 1:31a. Therefore, Man and the creation in which he lived, was morally "very good" in the eyes of God its Creator. However, Adam, as humanity's covenant head, rebelled against God. As God was to say later on to His people, "Like Adam, they transgressed the covenant; there they dealt treacherously with Me" Hosea 6:7 (margin, *cf.* Hosea 8:1b).

Good News

Scripture teaches that "Adam ... is a type of Him who was to come" Romans 5:14b. Thus Jesus Christ is the replacement "Adam" God sent into the world (see e.g., 1 Corinthians 15:45). Jesus is the new *federal representative* or *covenant head*. Through Adam's disobedience all humanity were made sinners (i.e., covenant breakers which is another way of saying that we are transgressors of God's Moral Law), but through Christ's obedience (i.e., His perfect keeping of the covenant's conditions and also paying the penalty owed for the breaking of it) those whom Christ represents are now righteous in God's eyes. The Gospel is the Good News that God has reconciled fallen man to Himself through the perfect works of Jesus Christ. This reconciliation is attained by the individual by grace through faith in the completed works of Christ (see e.g., Ephesians 2:8-9). Thus the Gospel.

Fallen World

The context for the aforementioned Good News (i.e., the Gospel) is that Man no longer lives in a morally "good" universe but a fallen world. This is not to say that creation itself became evil when Satan and subsequently Adam rebelled against God. For only moral agents (i.e., angels and human beings) can become evil.[11] God's Moral Law is spiritual (Romans 7:14). Thus morals are spiritual.

---

[11] Stars, planets, rocks, trees, dinosaurs, snakes, sharks, crocodiles, lions, tigers etc., are not inherently evil because they, (unlike fallen humans and fallen angels), are never disobedient to God's Covenant or Moral Law, i.e., the Ten Commandments. Only fallen humans and fallen angels are "moral agents." However, animals dangerous to humans are to be controlled, which may include putting the creature down should it maim or kill someone (Genesis 9:5; Exodus 21:28-32).

What happened when Adam sinned against God by consciously disobeying Him? Scripture says,

> For the creation was subjected to futility, not willingly, but because of Him who subjected *it* in hope; because the creation itself also will be delivered from the bondage of corruption into the glorious liberty of the children of God. For we know that the whole creation groans and labors with birth pangs together until now. Romans 8:20-22.

We see then that on account of Adam's sin everyone thereafter and we today live in a fallen world. Therefore, we ought to expect that at times things will go wrong for us. However, as human beings (i.e., as "moral agents"), we shall know both good and evil in the fallen world around us (Genesis 3:22a). (The "good" serves to remind us that God has not abandoned us. The "evil" or "bad" reminds us of our need for God's refuge and daily protection, as the Scripture reminds us, "Draw near to God and He will draw near to you" James 4:8a.)

Life's a Struggle

God had created Man as the pinnacle of His creation (see, e.g., Genesis 1:28), but when Adam sinned as Mankind's representative before God, we became distanced from our Maker. This (moral and therefore spiritual) separation caused it to become hard for Man to eke a living on and from the earth. It is worth quoting in full what the LORD God said to humanity's federal head,

Then to Adam He said, 'Because you have heeded the voice of your wife, and have eaten from the tree of which I commanded you, saying, "You shall not eat of it": 'Cursed *is* the ground for your sake; in toil you shall eat *of* it all the days of your life. Both thorns and thistles it shall bring forth for you, and you shall eat the herb of the field. In the sweat of your face you shall eat bread till you return to the ground, for out of it you were taken; for dust you *are,* and to dust you shall return.'"
Genesis 3:17-19.

Thus, life on earth is a struggle for all on earth; plants, animals and humans!

Fallen Man

Human nature has undergone a great transformation. We (collectively) have gone from being morally pure (pre-Fall) to morally corrupt (post-Fall). Another way of saying the same thing is that when Adam sinned we became spiritually dead. As the Scripture says, "The carnal mind is enmity against God; for it is not subject to the law of God, nor indeed can be" Romans 8:7.

The character of God is expressed in His Ten Commandments. Like a coin with the sovereign's head embossed on it, so God minted us as His own image and likeness. However, we are like old worn-out and tarnished pennies. It is hard to see the Moral

Law stamped on us. It is difficult for us to see it in ourselves. Thus, we make morally wrong choices.

Adam and Eve made a morally wrong choice, and all mankind thereafter suffered and still suffers Moral Injury unless and until God remedies it by grace through faith.

Moral Injury & Post Traumatic Stress

The Bible records the actions of Adam and Eve after they had, as moral agents, sinned against God. Their guilty consciences started accusing or excusing them as they tried to deal with their guilt and shift blame for what had happened away from themselves. Adam said to God, "The woman whom You gave to be with me, she gave me of the tree, and I ate" Genesis 3:12. Eve said, "The serpent deceived me, and I ate" Genesis 3:13b.

With Adam and Eve and their demise in mind let us remind ourselves of our definition of Moral Injury,

> Moral Injury is an inner conflict based on moral self assessment of having inflicted or failed to prevent significant harm. Its symptoms are excessive guilt, loss of meaning, anger and shame.

Some may wonder why God was so upset with Adam and Eve and why they were so upset with themselves simply for eating a piece of fruit. However, it was not that simple. God had given Adam and Eve (including us in them) as His moral agents the Great

Commission or Cultural Mandate, a portion of which is recorded in the following Scripture,

> So God created man in His *own* image; in the image of God He created him; male and female He created them. Then God blessed them, and God said to them, "Be fruitful and multiply; fill the earth and subdue it; have dominion over the fish of the sea, over the birds of the air, and over every living thing that moves on the earth. Genesis 1:27-28.

The command not to eat of the forbidden fruit of the tree of the knowledge of good and evil was merely an outward test to see if Adam as our representative would keep the Covenant, i.e., to see if Adam would remain obedient to God. Adam broke his probation and thereby forfeited the life that was promised him (and his descendants in him) for his obedience. Thus Adam by his action caused the deaths of every human being!

How did Adam and Eve set about dealing with their present demise? Did they immediately seek to draw near to God so that He would draw near to them? We need to remember that God had threatened Adam with death for disobeying Him (which conversely was the promise of life for obedience). As Scripture says,

> And the LORD God commanded the man, saying, "Of every tree of the garden you may freely eat; but of the tree of the knowledge of good and evil you shall not eat, for in the day

that you eat of it you shall surely die." Genesis
2:16-17.

What happened? Scripture says,

> So when the woman saw that the tree *was*
> good for food, that it *was* pleasant to the eyes,
> and a tree desirable to make *one* wise, she
> took of its fruit and ate. She also gave to her
> husband with her, and he ate. Genesis 3:6.

Upon eating the forbidden fruit Adam and Eve went
from loving God and their neighbour as themselves to
becoming totally self-conscious and self-absorbed
with their own problems. Thus, they began to suffer
Moral Injury – i.e., "excessive guilt, loss of meaning,
anger and shame." Quite possibly they also began to
suffer some form of Post-Traumatic Stress Disorder
(PTSD), which we have defined as, "A fear – victim
reaction to a perceived life threat. It has clinical
symptoms of flashbacks, nightmares, hyper-vigilance,
dissociation."

Anyway, Adam was afraid of God and what God was
going to do to him! But what did God do to Adam
and Eve? First, God came "looking" for them.

> Then the LORD God called to Adam and said
> to him, "Where *are* you?" So he said, "I heard
> Your voice in the garden, and I was afraid
> because I was naked; and I hid myself."
> Genesis 3:9-10.

Second, God spoke to the serpent, to Eve and to Adam, in that order. When speaking to the serpent God said,

> And I will put enmity between you and the woman, and between your seed and her Seed; He shall bruise your head, and you shall bruise His heel. Genesis 3:15.

Theologians refer to this as the *protevangelium*, i.e., the promise of the Gospel. Therefore, Adam and Eve heard the Good News (albeit in embryonic form). Third, God also showed Adam and Eve the Good News,

> Also for Adam and his wife the LORD God made tunics of skin, and clothed them. Genesis 3:21.

Conclusion

On account of the Fall, all of Mankind suffers Moral Injury. Moral Injury is spiritual. Those who have been diagnosed with Moral Injury, if they were not before, are now aware of their spiritual problem. God is able to heal Moral Injury – for good! Thus the Gospel.

Man: That Accusing Conscience

***"He who covers his sins will not prosper, but
whoever confesses and forsakes them will have
mercy."*** Proverbs 28:13

Introduction

All of us are guilty of trying to cover up our sins. An
example from the Bible would be David and his sins
with Bathsheba. David tried to cover up his sin of
adultery. He tried to manipulate Bathsheba's husband
Uriah. Uriah didn't cooperate the way David wanted
him to. Next thing David had Uriah sent to his certain
death. Sin is a lustful desire that begins in the heart.
Then, like a serpent, it slithers out from you. And
once it's out it's hard to put the lid on again – yet we
try! Sin truly is the opening up of a can of worms.
The more you try to cover up your sins the harder it
gets.

There's a certain amount of truth in the saying, "Give
a man enough rope and he's sure to hang himself."
We try to cover our sins because we don't want others
to find out about them. Maybe you don't want the
embarrassment. Maybe it's to protect your good
name. Maybe you're afraid you'll end up in prison.
But every last one of us who tries to cover our sins
knows this, that we are guilty! So we try to hide our
guilt.

Maybe you try to hide your guilt from the police. Maybe you try to hide your guilt from your neighbour, your family, mum and dad, husband or wife. But more than anything, we try to hide our guilt from ourselves! We'll even lie to ourselves in our attempt to escape our guilt!

We need to know that there is a proper and safe and most importantly, a biblical way to escape an accusing conscience. Otherwise we'll find life most difficult at times. It will be a struggle to *prosper*. And we don't necessarily mean prosper in the financial sense of the word. Here, we'll be talking more about the prosperity that comes with living with a guilt-free conscience.

In the following I'd like us to consider what it is we are actually doing when we try to cover our sins, when we should be confessing and forsaking them. We need to consider what is going on internally as well as externally. Sin is given birth in the mind and finds an outlet into the world through our bodies.

Adam lusted after the forbidden fruit and then tried to cover his sin with a fig leaf. In the following I want us to mainly focus on what is happening internally when we try to cover our sins. Therefore, we need to look at the conscience, for to cover your sins externally is simply the attempt to appease the internal conscience.

The general gist of what we're looking at is, *The way to remove the obstacle of an accusing conscience is to repent and believe in the Gospel.*

We'll look at three things to do with the conscience. We'll consider how the conscience works. This we'll deal with under the heading, *The Active Conscience.* Next, we'll see how the conscience accuses under the heading, *The Accusing Conscience.* And finally, we'll consider how the conscience may be silenced, *The Appeased Conscience.*

The Active Conscience

An active conscience is a conscience that either accuses or excuses you. Everyone has a conscience, though sometimes it's more active in some than others. But how does the conscience accuse? First we need to define what we mean by conscience. "SCIENCE" is to know and "CON" means together. Therefore literally "conscience" means "to know together." Hence to go against your conscience means that you do not have it all together, that you are in two minds about something. It means that something in your mind is gently nudging you. There are times when that something in your mind screams at you to – like a schoolteacher we once had – "Get back in line!"

The dictionary says that the conscience is: "[That] faculty by which distinctions are made between moral right and wrong." Therefore, the conscience is a built-in gauge all of us have. It measures right and wrong. Or, if you will, it's a little policeman each of us carries around with us. He blows his whistle when we're about to do something wrong. Then he comes and thumps on our door after we ignore him.

What about the flash of guilt when the police point their radar gun at your car? Your mind starts to go into overdrive as your try to think of an excuse! I was stopped in Toronto back in 1977 just after Canada had switched to metric. "Officer, my speedometer still works on the old scale!" "Well maybe this ticket will help you learn arithmetic!"

The conscience is that aspect of us which says, "I shouldn't have thought/said/done that!" We hardly know our conscience is there until it points its accusing radar gun at us! This is what you call a pang of guilty conscience. When you think about it, God knows all about the skeletons in your closet. As we try to cover our sins we may end up wrestling our conscience for years on end. However, you should know that the conscience only accuses when there is something wrong.

Our conscience speaks to us and says, "You've got a problem here." It might be instantaneous, "The checkout chick undercharged you for the dog food. Tell her!" Or your conscience may remind you of something from years ago. "What about the time you cheated on the school exam?" "What about that income tax return you lodged?" "What about that used car you sold?" Well, that's the policeman knocking on your door.

A person can wrestle for years with the guilt of sin. Perhaps a lie they told that caused pain and anguish to others. Perhaps it was something they stole. Perhaps it was some extra-marital affair they had. Whatever! We never really notice our conscience when we are doing the right thing. It excuses us (Romans 2:15). It only accuses us when we go against it, when we cross it!

I once worked for a company that seldom commended anyone for doing a good job. However, if anyone did anything wrong, they were condemned. That company, like your conscience, always expects you to do the right thing. God commands that everyone be perfect as He is perfect. That's why He made us in His own image and likeness, perfect! We are supposed to reflect Him. Hence God has given each of us a conscience to keep us in line.

The conscience measures our actions against our highest morals. If you have a low set of morals, your conscience will let you away with more. The highest set of morals are God's Ten Commandments, the summary of God's Law.

Now, being made in the image and likeness of God means that we also have God's Decalogue stamped on our heart. Christian or no, it doesn't matter, all mankind has the Decalogue engraved on its heart. Romans 2:15 tells us we show by our actions that we have God's Law written on our heart. In other words, each of us has a copy of God's code of conduct nailed to the wall of our heart. Yes, the print is obscured by sin, like the house rules on the wall of a grubby pub! Nicotine stains, beer stains, blood stains from pub-brawls make it harder to read the notice on the wall. And the more intoxicated the person is, the less he tends to care about the rules.

Society behaves much like a drunk regarding God's Law. It tends to use the Decalogue as he would a pub dartboard. Now society does collectively what we do as individuals. Society as a whole tries to muzzle the little policeman whose station is in the head. But what about the practicing Christian? He has more than the little policeman. The Christian has the indwelling of the Holy Spirit (Romans 8:9-11). Therefore the Christian has a more difficult time trying to silence his conscience. The Christian becomes guilty of grieving and even quenching the Spirit if He ignores God's Commandments. As the Prophet Micah says, "[The] LORD Has shown you, O man, what is good."

When we do the right thing we are doing what is good. When we don't do what is good we begin to hear from our conscience.

The Accusing Conscience
To talk about the accusing conscience is to talk about feelings of guilt. Guilt can be a real thorn in the flesh. None of us likes the feeling of guilt. So we try to appease our accusing conscience, which is to say in the words of Proverbs 28:13 that we try to "cover our sins."

What is sin? "Sin is any want of conformity unto, or transgression of, the law of God." Westminster Shorter Catechism question and answer 14. Sin is any failure to measure up to what God requires, or disobedience to His commands. Sin is disobeying or not conforming to God's Law in any way.

As we sense the guilt of sin, we may try to rationalise our sin. We can become preoccupied with our sense of guilt. John MacArthur Jnr. says,

> Deep in our hearts, we all know something is desperately wrong with us. Our conscience constantly confronts us with our own sinfulness. Try as we might to blame others, or seek psychological explanations for how we feel, we cannot escape reality. We cannot ultimately deny our own consciences. We feel guilt, and we know the horrible truth about who we are on the inside.[12]

The Puritan Richard Sibbes wrote in the 17th century, "The conscience is the soul reflecting upon itself."[13] The conscience, then, is you taking the measuring stick to everything you think, say, or do.

---

[12] John F, MacArthur Jnr., Wayne A, Mack and the Master's College Faculty, *Biblical Counseling, A Basic Guide to the Principles and Practices of Counseling,* Word Publishing, Dallas, 1994, 104.
[13] John F. MacArthur Jnr., (as quoted) *The Vanishing Conscience*, Word Press, Dallas, 1995, 36.

Yet we try to reason with our conscience as we try to rationalise our sin. We think things like, "It wasn't really my fault!" "If only he or she had done this or that!" "If only he or she had been somewhere else!" "If only – if only – if only…"

Sometimes a person cannot get on with their life because of an accusing conscience. They can go over the same old argument day in day out, day after day *ad nauseam* as they try to get rid of the feeling of guilt. David the Psalmist puts it like this in Psalm 32:3-4,

> When I kept silent, my bones grew old through my groaning all the day long. For day and night Your hand was heavy upon me; my vitality was turned into the drought of summer.

David was trying to cover his sins. He was trying to conceal them. And all he did was groan all day long! That Puritan Sibbes compared the chastisement of a violated conscience to "a flash of Hell!"[14] When you think about it, Hell is the place where people are preoccupied with a guilty conscience forever! But, as Sibbes says, we here only experience a flash of Hell!

Occasionally there's a report on the news of someone turning themselves in to the police. Perhaps someone who has robbed a bank, or murdered someone, or whatever. It can be something they did years ago, decades. I remember seeing one about a woman who

---

[14] Ibid., 40.

had committed a crime back in 1970. However, her conscience finally got the better of her. She couldn't handle its accusations any longer. So she turned herself in!

We cannot handle an accusing conscience. An accusing conscience is something like a sewer. An accusing conscience reminds us of something vile sludging around beneath the surface. In big cities occasionally a sewer will explode! Methane gas can build up, and if it ignites then Whammo! A heavy manhole cover can fly into the air. Well, in a similar way some people just seem to explode.

Feelings of guilt can cause a person to act in all sorts of abnormal ways. And our verse is telling us that we won't prosper when guilt is weighing us down. It's like Christian in Pilgrim's Progress whose burden was a backpack full of guilt that needed to be gotten rid of.

Now, guilt can be felt for a variety of reasons. But every single one of those reasons has to do with right and wrong. In other words, guilt always has to do with morals. This is because the conscience only accuses when there is something wrong.

What if, what if, what if it is you yourself who has been wronged? What if you are blaming yourself for some terrible thing that happened to you? What if you are carrying the guilt of having been abused as a child? "If only, if only, if only I had done what I was told." Well, there are at least two ways we can look at this:

1. You can plead your innocence before God.
2. You can continue to reason with your conscience.

Surely the right thing to do is to plead your case before God. God knows what happened to you. If you're innocent, He knows it. He saw it. And the main thing that matters is that God knows that it was you who were wronged. But then there is option 2, which is no option, is it? For option 2. is to continue to reason with your conscience. And if you do that you will continue tormenting yourself.

But here's something worth considering, and this is where it gets really difficult. It is sometimes possible that we blame God for something terrible that happened to us. "God, why did You let this happen to me?" Now, if we keep in mind that our conscience only accuses us when there is something wrong, we won't go too far wrong here.

Think about it, it is always wrong to blame God for sin, our sins or the sins of another. God is not the author of sin. God never sins against us. If a person was, let's say, sexually abused as a child, that person shouldn't blame him- or herself. But neither should they blame God. God hates sin! To be sure, the police should be called, and child abusers ought to be arrested. And I know that there is no great solace in knowing that the abuser's conscience will be accusing night and day. However, it's true.

The Appeased Conscience
How is an accusing conscience silenced? Well, in a word, whenever your conscience accuses you of anything, even something of which you claim to be innocent, see that as your cue to plead before God. In other words, flee to God for refuge every time a pang of conscience hits. Continue to do this and your problem, whatever it is, will leave you. Therefore, run to God for mercy. Now, this doesn't mean that you just pay God lip service. It doesn't mean, "O, I tried that, but it doesn't work." Fleeing to God means begging Him for mercy.

Nowadays if someone has a pang of guilt we tend to say, "Don't be so hard on yourself." We might say, "You need to talk to someone about your problem." And maybe so. But it is God we need to talk to. We need to talk to God, not the butcher, the baker, and the candlestick maker. God! Not the priest, the psychologist, the shrink. God! To be sure, a problem shared is a problem halved. So there is some benefit in talking to others about our problems with guilt. However, we need to seek audience with God, and not just to pay Him lip service.

Do you remember the Parable about the Pharisee and Tax Collector? The Pharisee prayed something to the effect, "God, I thank You that I'm so wonderful! I'm a super faster and a brilliant tither. I'm not like other people at all. In my own eyes I deserve better than this. But here I am stuck among a bunch of sinners including this debauched tax-collector!" Is this what we mean by fleeing to God? God forbid! Fleeing to God is pleading for His mercy when you are wracked with guilt and anguish of soul. Fleeing to God is the prayer of the Tax-collector, "God be merciful to me a sinner!" Fleeing to God is repentance. It is turning your back on sin.

You are sinning if you keep on wrestling with your conscience when you should be seeking God. But instead of fleeing to God we tend to keep on going over the same old thing in our head. And when we do this we cannot truly get on with life, because we're too busy wrestling with our conscience.

It's like Tarzan wrestling with a snapping crocodile! We're forever splashing around in the depths of our sins. We are too busy trying to cover our sins without God! But look at Proverbs 28:13, "Whoever confesses and forsakes his sins will have mercy." It doesn't say perhaps will have mercy. It says you WILL have mercy! Mercy from what? Mercy from the Hell you've been having flashes of!

When you flee to God with your pangs of conscience you are fleeing from Hell. The Word says we are to repent, that is, we are to change our minds. Our minds are no longer to be split in two as we go against our conscience. But rather we are to turn our back on our sins – all sin. The Proverb says, "Confess them and forsake them."

Look at the Proverb again as we try to tie it all together: "He who covers his sins will not prosper, but whoever confesses and forsakes them will have mercy" Proverbs 28:13. We've seen that to cover your sins is the same as trying to appease a guilty conscience. I hope that has become clear to you, if it wasn't before. But what would happen if someone covered your sins for you? Would that appease your conscience? Well, that's exactly what's happening when you keep on confessing and keep on forsaking your sins. It means that someone else is covering your sins for you. Why? Because this means that you are asking God to be merciful and cover your sins for you. And God by His grace and His mercy clears you of your guilt, even your guilty conscience. For that's what happens when you confess your sins. You are exposing it for God to deal with it. And if you are coming before God with your sins, then you should know that God has already dealt with your sins, and He has already cleared you of the guilt of that sin. As John MacArthur puts it,

> True guilt has only one cause, and that is sin.
> And sin…is the very thing the gospel is given
> to conquer.[15]

The Gospel is the Good News of the Grace and Mercy of God in Jesus Christ. It's the good news that Jesus Christ has delivered us from all our sins. It is the good news that He has conquered sin. It is the Good News that He has covered our sins – with His own shed blood. Christ takes away all our guilt. Yes,

---

[15] John MacArthur, *Biblical Counseling,* 104.

even the feelings of guilt. Therefore continue to confess yours sins to God through Jesus Christ and God will have mercy on you and grant you a clear conscience.

Conclusion

Christ's shed blood sprinkles our hearts "from an evil conscience" Hebrews 10:22. His blood protects us from all accusations – even the accusations of Satan. So, the next time your conscience accuses you, flee to God with it! Don't wrestle with it. Do what the Proverb says, confess it and forsake it. The more you do that, the less your conscience will accuse you. For "He who covers his sins will not prosper, but whoever confesses and forsakes them will have mercy."

God: The Healer

"Come now, and let us reason together,"
says the LORD, *"Though your sins are like scarlet,*
they shall be as white as snow; though they are red
like crimson, they shall be as wool." Isaiah 1:18

Introduction

Notice what the LORD is saying in this verse. Almighty God is inviting us to *reason* with Him. He is inviting us to confess our sins to Him and have Him forgive us for them. However, more importantly, God is saying that He will forgive you your wrongdoings! Like removing our backpacks after a long foot-blistering hike we are to unburden ourselves of our load of sins. As we hand over our sins to God, He takes away our guilt and our shame. This in turn results in us no longer having to struggle with a guilty conscience. Thus we move from Moral Injury to Moral Repair.

A Reasonable Faith

It stands to reason that if God wants us to reason with Him then first we must believe, (i.e., have faith) that He exists. The writer to the Hebrews says, "But without faith *it is* impossible to please *Him,* for he who comes to God must believe that He is, and *that* He is a rewarder of those who diligently seek Him" Hebrews 11:6. Think about it, the reward for diligently seeking God (among other things) is peace of mind, i.e., the removal of a guilty conscience.

Some people have actually said to me, "I wish I had *your* faith." Well, according to the Bible every human being believes in God. We simply suppress that knowledge through our own wickedness. To say that we know God is simply another way of saying that everyone begins with the presupposition that God exists. Each of us inherently knows that God exists because God has built it into our being. We are made in His own image and likeness. From here it is simply a matter of what people do with that congenital presupposition that results on whether they will end up with a clear conscience or not.

Almighty God your Maker is inviting you to reason with Him. However, it stands to reason that you would not be reasoning together with God if He is absent from the conversation or dialogue, absent from your thoughts. Strange as it may seem, this is the way that some people treat God, as if He is simply a mathematical abstraction or philosophical equation and not the *personal* Triune God who created us in His own image and likeness. It is because God is a *Person*, (actually God is three Persons, i.e., the Father, the Son or Word, and the Holy Spirit, Matthew 28:19), that we are able to have a *personal* conversation with Him.

Jesus says, "No one comes to the Father except through Me" John 14:6. We speak to the Father in the power of the Spirit through the Son and God speaks to us by His Spirit with His Word. In other words, we pray to Him and He replies to us through His Word, the Bible.

But again, notice that we are not speaking into the void. We are not calling out in an empty building, "Is there anyone there?" God is! And He is everywhere at once. We are to reason with God, the God who is there! Think about it, if you do not believe that God exists then why would your conscience be troubling you? Why do I ask this? Well, your conscience is part, a big part, of one of the ways that God is using to make His existence known to you. This has to do with you being made in His image. As a mirror would not reflect your image unless you existed, so you and I would not be the image and likeness of God if He did not exist. However, God through His Word, the Bible, says that we are His likeness. "With the tongue we praise our Lord and Father, and with it we curse men, who have been made in God's likeness" James 3:9. Like a "Hall of Mirrors" our own sin distorts us individually as the image of God. Therefore, none of us (apart from Jesus) gives His true reflection.

A Reflecting Faith
Wrestling with one's own conscience (a prominent symptom of Moral Injury) is a first step on the road towards reasoning with God. Feelings of guilt come about when one has failed or is failing to measure up to one's own idea of moral good. The conscience is the measuring stick whereby we determine how far we are short of the mark. "For all have sinned and fall short of the glory of God" Romans 3:23.

Let us once again reflect on what Richard Sibbes said: "The conscience is the soul reflecting upon itself." Note the difference between the soul reflecting upon itself and wrestling with one's own conscience. Whereas the former is you reasoning with yourself, the latter is you arguing with yourself! Isn't it better simply to examine your own reflection than to attack it like some angry bird attacking its reflection in a windowpane?

Here's the rub: Healing begins for the individual when he or she recognizes that Moral Injury, like its sibling PTSD, is a *spiritual* problem. Now it becomes easier to see one of the reasons why Western psychiatry and psychology are having so much trouble healing people suffering from the symptoms of PTSD and Moral Injury. These systems are based on an Atheistic premise which denies the existence of soul and/or spirit as commonly taught in the Bible and Christianity. The Bible says, "But the natural man does not receive the things of the Spirit of God, for they are foolishness to him; nor can he know *them,* because they are spiritually discerned." 1 Corinthians 2:14. The bottom line is that spiritual things (including spiritual problems such as PTSD and Moral Injury) are spiritually discerned.

Now, this is not to say that modern psychiatrists and psychologists can offer no help to their patients. However, like any other science that detaches itself from God and His Biblical revelation, they are missing the key component of what they are dealing with, which is God and that which is His image, i.e., human beings.

One discerning doctor I was talking to about PTSD said, "You know? PTSD is so hard to fix because we're dealing with something invisible!" Think about it, we only know that a person is suffering from PTSD or Moral Injury by way of revelation. If that sounds too Biblical then let me state it in another way. We only know that PTSD and Moral Injury exist because someone has told us about them. We cannot see, hear, taste, smell or touch PTSD and Moral Injury. They remain invisible until someone reveals them to us.

If this is beginning to sound a bit like gobbledegook to you then I would suggest that it is because Western Science has had some success in trying to extricate itself from the science of Theology. This is what I mean by Atheistic science. It follows a Materialist philosophy and it ignores and even denies that which is spiritual. Therefore, the road to recovery for those suffering PTSD and Moral Injury (and Western Science itself!) is a return to the inclusion of Theology in scientific discussion instead of its present ostracism.

"God is Spirit." John 4:24. And a human being is a soul-spirit with a body. (2 Thessalonians 5:23). God is invisible (Colossians 1:15) and so is the spirit and the soul of a human being. God is the Father and the Son/Word and the Holy Spirit (Matthew 28:19). "The Word became flesh" John 1:14, which is to say that Jesus is God and also is a soul-spirit with a body, i.e., a human being like us. How do we know that Jesus is

God? The same way we know that someone has PTSD or Moral Injury. Revelation!

We believe you (i.e., we have *faith*) when you tell us that you have PTSD and/or Moral Injury, but we believe you only on account of what you tell us. There is no other way of our knowing and believing you. PTSD and or Moral Injury remain invisible to others until and unless you reveal it to them. It's a faith thing! We either believe you or don't believe you. "Now faith … is the evidence of things not seen." Hebrews 11:1 (abrev.)

John Cantwell rose from the rank of a Private to a Major General in the Australian Army. He was involved in conflicts in Iraq and Afghanistan. He wrote a book describing the lead up to his suffering from post-traumatic stress disorder (PTSD). Clearly he also suffers from Moral Injury, for in that same book his wife, Jane, is quoted as saying,

> And guilt—he felt responsible for the deaths of some young American soldiers who'd been killed by a roadside bomb. I told him over and over that he'd had to make a choice, that it wasn't his fault. He'd just stare out at the waves and say, 'Yes, it was my fault.'[16]

Because PTSD and Moral Injury are spiritual, we are only offering band-aid solutions until we acknowledge the "Father of spirits" (Hebrews 12:9)

---

[16] John Cantwell, *Exit Wounds – One Australian's War On Terror*, Kindle Edition, Melbourne University Publishing, 2013.

and ask Him, nay, beg Him to intervene and heal us. Spiritual healing is the gracious healing of our spirit by God's Spirit. God heals even those who are truly guilty! Once healed, as the writer to the Hebrews says, "Pray for us. We are sure that we have a clear conscience and desire to live honourably in every way" Hebrews 13:18.

Dear sufferer of PTSD and/or Moral Injury. My prayer for you is that your suffering will end and your conscience will become clear by continuously encountering God in Jesus Christ His only Son and receiving the forgiveness that He purchased for all who would put their trust in Him as the Holy Spirit applies it to you.

Conclusion

The first step toward being healed of your PTSD and/or Moral Injury is to acknowledge that as a human being you are God's moral agent by His creation, and as such you have broken His Moral law and need to seek and to receive His forgiveness.

The second step is to acknowledge that God has made you like Him, i.e., triune in Nature. You are body and soul and spirit, i.e., a soul-spirit with a body, and as such and with God's enabling are able to dialogue (i.e., reason) with Him.

The third step is to acknowledge that you, like the rest of humanity, as a human being are fallen in nature. There already is something morally wrong with you from conception and birth. This is discovered with the first pang of conscience!

The fourth step is to acknowledge that your accusing conscience is revelation of that which is spiritual, i.e., God and the human soul and spirit. It lets us know that something is wrong with you and that you need God the Spirit's help and healing.

The fifth step is to acknowledge that God alone can fully heal us. He is willing if you are!

The sixth step is the following exposition explaining how God removes our sins through Jesus Christ and what He did on the cross.

Jesus: The Sin Removalist

"The next day John saw Jesus coming towards him, and said, 'Behold! The Lamb of God who takes away the sin of the world.'" John 1:29

Introduction

Jesus is referred to by various descriptive names in the Bible. In one place the Apostle Paul refers to Jesus as "Our Passover." In another place Jesus refers to Himself as the bread from heaven. He calls Himself the Vine and also the Good Shepherd who lays down His life for His sheep. He says elsewhere, "I am the door." We see in the verse of Scripture before us that Jesus is called the Lamb of God. Therefore, it would be good to do what John Baptiser is inviting us to do. There's Jesus walking towards you. Look at Him as He draws nearer to you.

Now, if you're anything like me, you'll have a load of sin you'll be wanting rid of. And, since Jesus is the Lamb of God who takes away the sin of the world, who better than Jesus is there to take away your sins from you?

The general gist of what we're looking at in the following is this: *Keep on handing over your sins to Jesus Christ the Sin Removalist.*

The Pick-up

Each of us has a load of sin we need removed. According to the Bible we live in a world full of sin[17]

---

[17] Romans 8:20-22.

and that each one of us is full of sin.[18] Now, when the Garbos[19] go on strike the garbage piles up in the street! Sometimes the garbage piles so high the Government has to send in the army to remove it. Sin is the pile of rotting Garbage that comes between us and God. And God won't come near us until the garbage and its stench is removed. Therefore God sent His Son Jesus Christ to remove the sin of the world. God loaded the sins of His people onto the back of His Son. Then God incinerated our sin. The incinerator is Calvary's cross. God poured out His fiery wrath upon His Son as He hung on a cross with all our sin. Jesus Christ, then, is the *Sin Removalist!*

Now then, since each one of us contributes to the sin of the world, each of us has a load of sin that needs to be incinerated on Christ's cross. We know that Christ died for the sins of His people over 2000 years ago. I wasn't around then and neither were you. However, Scripture tells us that Jesus Christ is the same yesterday, today and forever.[20] Therefore we today can look to Him and seek Him to take away our sins for us. Otherwise, at the end of your life you'll be left with a pile of rotten sin on your back with no one to remove it. And, according to Scripture, the God who hates all sin will pour His fiery wrath upon you. Horrible as it sounds, this means that you will be incinerated forever, which means eternal conscious torment in the fires of hell!

---

[18] Romans 3:23; Galatians 3:22.
[19] Australian term for garbage-collectors.
[20] Hebrews 13:8.

Now, I know that hell is not a popular subject nowadays. And who likes talking about a place about which Jesus says, "It is better for you to enter the kingdom of God with one eye, than having two eyes, to be cast into hell fire – where their worm does not die and the fire is not quenched" Mark 9:47. It's a picture of the dump outside of the city of Jerusalem. The carcasses and the offal of the sacrificed animals were thrown into the dump and burnt. Those carcasses around the edge of the fire were full of worms and maggots. It's a horrible thought and who in their right mind would want to spend an eternity there, especially those who have seen the Lamb who takes away the sin of the world! But it's all to do with sin, isn't it? – the sin of unbelief which is prevalent today.

Think about it, every time you break even the least of God's commandments you are throwing another piece of rotten garbage on the street! And, just as you can be fined if caught littering on the street, so God holds each one of us accountable for every one of our sins. However, the penalty is not a slap on the wrist. *And what is sin?* "Sin is the want of conformity unto, or transgression of, any law of God, given as a rule to the reasonable creature."[21]

I'm sure you reckon that you are a reasonable creature. You have the God given ability to reason whether something's right or wrong. And of course we apply our reasoning in light of what the Bible says is right and wrong. We measure whether a thing is

---

[21] Westminster Larger Catechism Q&A 24.

right or wrong against what God says in His Word.

Now let's test our ability to reason: *Is it right or wrong to murder your next door neighbour?* Instead of borrowing sugar, you kill him for no reason, is that a right or wrong thing to do? It's a wrong thing to do, isn't it? But what makes it wrong? If you are one of those who been brought up to think we were not created by God to be His image but that we all evolved accidently from slime, you'll have some trouble answering that question. How can it be morally wrong to rearrange a bunch of chemicals, i.e., murder someone – if that's all we are? Well, the Bible says God designed and made us in His own moral image. So, we're not a bunch of atoms and gases that accidentally bumped into each other one dark night. Therefore it's wrong to murder your neighbour because God who made us says so.

So, let me state again that sin is ANY failure to measure up to whatever God requires, or any disobedience to any of His commands given as a rule for creatures with reason. Does that sound reasonable to you? We all know about the sins we see each other do outwardly. But what about those sins we commit inwardly? What about those invisible sins, the ones that no one else can see? No one but God that is. There's a spiritual dimension to sin then.

You're sinning inwardly by hating someone in your heart. You're committing murder in your heart. You're sinning inwardly or spiritually by lusting after another's wife or husband. You're committing adultery with him or her in your heart. I can't see what goes on in your heart, but God can. However, I know that I sometimes pile up garbage in my own heart. How about you? I've got one or two old banana skins in my heart. They cause me to slip from time to time. Therefore, I need to watch out for the Sin Removalist and have Him take them away.

What was the first piece of garbage to be produced in the world? It was a piece of rotten fruit, wasn't it? It wasn't rotten when it was hanging on the tree of the knowledge of good and evil in the Garden. But it started to rot when Adam sunk his pearly-whites into it. God had told Adam not to eat the fruit of that tree. Did Adam listen? No! So the rotten garbage of sin began to pile up.

As Adam and Eve had children it began to pile up more and more in the streets of the world. It was Adam then, who produced the first load of rotten garbage.[22] And each one of his descendants all the way down to you and me have added to it.[23] The sin of the world, then, is the sin that separates us from God. And the garbage dump is a place full of filth and disease. And so became the world after Adam disobeyed God. However, God sent His beloved Son into the world to remove the world's garbage. So, Christ is the Sin Removalist who takes away the stinking load. "Behold! The Lamb of God who takes away the sin of the world."

---

[22] Genesis 3:11.
[23] Romans 5:12f.

Truth be known, we can hardly move for the amount of sin around the place. Sin restricts us. It trips us up. We fall over it. We even wallow in it like a pig in mud. Even those good things we try to do are to God like filthy rags![24] As Job says, "Who can bring a clean thing out of an unclean? No one!" Job 14:4. A world full of sin cannot produce something untainted by sin, can it? So how are we to get back to a Holy, Righteous, Sinless and Perfect God? Well, the only way back to the presence of God and Paradise is for Him to come and remove our load, i.e., our load of sin.

When I lived in Canada I had a friend who had his own garbage removal business. I gave him a hand for a few days. It was nothing like what we now have here in Brisbane Australia, you know, where the guy sits in his cabin and the big arms pick up your wheelie-bin. No! Back then wheelie bins hadn't caught on in Canada yet. So what we had to do was run after the garbage truck and throw the garbage bags into the back of it! I did this for three days one hot summer. Yuk! (And the pay was even worse!) But anyway, he sometimes got called out at night to pick up a dead deer or elk or even a moose from lying in the middle of the road. I gave him a hand one night to manhandle a dead white-tailed deer into the back of his wagon. I was thankful that it was the freezing cold winter and not the roasting hot summer. For you know how terrible is the smell of a rotten carcass in summer! Well, the sin of the world has the stench of death clinging to it. The trouble is that we're so used

---

[24] Isaiah 64:6.

to the smell that we hardly even notice it. However, the Son of God came willingly to take away the sin of the world. God loaded the sin of the world onto His Son's back.

Jesus became the scapegoat for all those who lay their sins upon Him. The Bible illustrates it like this: In Leviticus 16:6 we're told that once a year, "Aaron the high priest, shall take from the congregation of the children of Israel two kids of the goats as a sin offering." And according to Exodus 12:5 it was permissible to use either a young sheep or goat. Sometimes it's really hard to tell the difference between a sheep and a goat anyhow. Anyway, the sheep or goat had to be without a blemish on it. Then lots would be drawn to decide which of the two would get to do what. One of the animals would be sacrificed as a sin offering required by God, while the other would be set free in the wilderness.

Now, both the scapegoat and the sacrificial goat picture what Jesus did as the Lamb of God. Take the scapegoat. Israel would confess her sins before God. Then the high priest would lay his hands on the head of the goat. As he held its horns the sin of the people would symbolically be transferred or imputed onto the back of the goat. The young goat or sheep would be led into the wilderness. It was the lamb that takes away the sin of the people. It was their scapegoat. Of course, it didn't really take away their sin. The scapegoat just reminded them of their need to have their sins removed. And as for the other young sheep or goat, well, after the sin of the people was symbolically transferred or imputed to it, it was sacrificed.

Now then, it's not hard to see how this applies to Jesus. Think about the time when Jesus was baptized by John. Mark 1:4-5 says, "John came baptizing in the wilderness and preaching a baptism of repentance for the remission of sins. And all the land of Judea, and those from Jerusalem, went out to Him and were all baptized by him in the Jordan River, confessing their sins."

So get the picture, the people of God are confessing their sins. And having water applied to them as a picture of the washing away of the filth and stench of sin. And then we read in John 1:29, "The next day John saw Jesus coming toward him, and said, 'Behold! The Lamb of God who takes away the sin of the world!" After Jesus was baptized with water and with the Holy Spirit, Mark in his Gospel says in 1:12, "Immediately the Spirit drove Him into the wilderness." Therefore Jesus fulfilled the role of the Old Testament scapegoat.

But what about the other young goat or sheep that was to be sacrificed? Well, Jesus fulfilled that role too, didn't He? The justice of God demands that our sins be paid for, either by you or a substitute. Christ is our scapegoat who takes away our sin. And He is our sacrificial Lamb who pays the debt we owe to God for our sin. So then, we've seen that Jesus Christ is the Sin Removalist. And each of us needs Him to pick up our sins and take them away. Even as we have our garbage picked up and taken away.

Now we need to consider the place where Jesus went when He took away our sins.

The Delivery

Jesus took away our sins upon the cross, didn't He? My friend, the one who owned his own garbage truck, had to go to the city dump every time his truck was full. He would take the Perimeter Highway which had to be the bumpiest road in Winnipeg! Before they would let him into the dump they would get him to drive unto a platform. They would weigh the contents of his truck and charge him certain dumping fees according to the weight of his load. Jesus had the weight of the world's sin upon Him. And the price He had to pay to dump our sin was death (as per the wages of sin[25]).

The bumpy road to the cross was slow and painful for Jesus. Behold! The Lamb of God betrayed and arrested in the Garden of Gethsemane! Behold! The Lamb of God as they took Him away to sacrifice Him. Behold Him as they paraded Him down the street. Behold Him as they spat upon Him as He walked along the road to His death. Behold Him as His legs buckled under the weight of our sin, your sin and my sin. Behold Him as He set His face to take the muck and filth of our sin to deliver it to the city dump.

If you want to see what it's like to be in hell then look

---

[25] Romans 6:23.

no further than Christ on the cross. Listen to a Man whose soul feels forsaken by God. Hear Him cry out, "My God, My God why have You forsaken Me? ... My strength is dried up like a potsherd, and My tongue clings to My jaws; You have brought Me to the dust of death" Psalm 22:1,15.

But see if you can catch His eye before He goes there. See if you can catch His eye as He walks along the road. See if you can get Him to take your sin with Him to the dump too! If you can see Him, you won't be too late to catch Him. He won't race away. He'll wait for you. That's why He came. He came to take away the sin of the world.

Confess your sins and repent of them. Place them on the back of Jesus as He struggles up Calvary's hill. Only He can bear your sins. He can bear the sin of the whole world! But you have to behold Him in order for Him to take away your sins.

What's it like when you forget to put out the garbage and you miss the garbage collection? You're left with a bin full of garbage and you have to try to dump it by yourself, don't you? I remember when we were out in Springsure (Central Queensland) I missed the garbage collection. Of course it was about 40 degrees Celsius in the shade. So I loaded the maggot infested garbage into the church's new car and drove along the dusty road to the village dump.

Jesus Christ carried our sin on His back and He walked to the city dump. He made one trip and one trip alone when He went to the cross with our sin. But let's say a person missed out on Jesus taking away his sin. Let's say this person was you. Would you be happy to deal with your own sin? What do you think will happen when you get to the city dump? (For that is where God will send you.) What will you do with all your sin when you are weighed on the weigh scales? What will you use for money to pay to dump your sins when all you have with you is garbage? What will you do when you've used up all the credit God has given you and now at the end of your life He's demanding payment, full payment?

God demands the penalty of death for sin and there you and I are sitting with a whole life full of it! So it's a bit useless to say that you don't have any sin since God is weighing you on the scales. And the trouble is that God demands payment for even the smallest of sins – the payment is death. Look at Jesus on the cross if you don't believe me – that's the price of sin! And the sin He had wasn't even His sin for He was sinless! No, it was the sin of all those who look to Jesus to be delivered from their sins. It's better to catch the eye of Jesus and have Him take your sins away now, because if you die without them being removed, you'll spend eternity paying for them. However, always remember that God forgives those who have had their sin removed by the Sin Removalist.

What's it like then to have your sins forgiven? Well, Romans 8:1 says, "There is therefore now no condemnation to those who are in Christ Jesus." We know we are in Christ Jesus, and we know our sins have been taken away, when we are beholding Christ. When you keep on looking for Christ and keep on looking to Christ you know you haven't missed the Sin Removalist. For He is the Lamb of God who takes away the sin of the world!

Conclusion

Always remember that Jesus is The Sin Removalist. He is the One who has picked-up the sins of those who keep on keeping their eyes on Him. He is the One who has delivered us from our sins by taking them to Calvary's cross. So keep on beholding the Lamb of God who takes away the sin of the world. And, to keep your conscience clear, as you become aware of them, keep on handing over your sins to Jesus Christ the Sin Removalist.

Me: A Personal Application

"He restores my soul; He leads me in the paths of righteousness for His name's sake" Psalm 23:3.

Introduction

I found it cathartic to confess my own and personal moral injury to others. I posted some of the following on my Blog site for the whole world to see! And it felt really good. It was as if a stagnant and dead pond had been flushed out with clean fresh water and restocked with life. I was finally free of a rusty ball-and-chain that I had been dragging around for years!

Childhood Memories

I was asked to fill out an online questionnaire. It was about health and wellbeing. I was doing quite well until I got to the bit where I was asked to list any traumatic events I had experienced in my life and how they might have affected me.

I went through the agony of vividly replaying in my mind, watching as a five or six year old, another child of the same age being slowly crushed to death against a brick wall by a wheel rim of a slow moving lorry (truck). Blood! The child had tried to squeeze through the gap as the truck tried to manoeuvre around a corner where we were. Painful memories. Tears! Aaargh!!!

The survey also went on to ask: Other than rape, were you sexually assaulted or molested? What? I've only just recently started to talk about this upon hearing about someone else's demise. The other person had been raped. The survey asked at what age did sexual molestation begin for me and at what age did it end? And how many times was I sexually molested? Tearing up once more I wracked my brains to recall events from fifty-plus years before! I suppose it was between the ages of ten and twelve. Maybe thirty times? But it was probably more, much more!

It's Not My Fault!
I'd been walking around with this smelly sludge sloshing around in the dark bilges of my mind from pre to post pubescence! Yes, I had told my wife about it years ago and maybe one of my sisters a few years ago. But that was about it until recently. Recently I have told three or four others about this. Man, speaking about it made me feel better! None of it was my fault!

But back to the survey… The questionnaire asked how these painful memories were affecting me. Through the tears I ticked the appropriate boxes as I sobbed and blew into tissues. Then running both eyes over the page again in order to make sure I had answered all the questions I was ready to move on to the next page. I pressed the button on the screen hoping the questions on the next page would be somewhat less painful than what I had just gone through. No-o-o! It wanted me to "sign in" again. Somehow all the previous data had been irretrievably lost!

My intention was to try again the next day, but I was not looking forward to going through all of those painful questions again. But then again, upon reflection, talking about it helped me to face up to my demons… Begone! Alas! Tomorrow came and went as have many tomorrows. I'm not happy with the callous way the survey treated me.

No Malice!

Yes, I found recalling being sexually molested for a couple or more years from between the ages of ten and thirteen by one man in particular (though I recall also one of two of his mates availed themselves of me). Let me say for the record, and this is important for you the reader to know, that I do not recall there being any penetration involved. Let me say also that I hold no hatred toward these men. The main perpetrator is dead and I can't even remember who the other guys were!

I hold no malice towards these men. Sure, if the police had apprehended them and charged them, I would wish them dealt with to the full measure of the law. However, I store no hatred towards them in my heart. If any of them had asked with full repentance for my forgiveness I would have given it to them.

But there was something more troubling to me.

The Lie!

My mum and dad had asked me on different occasions if "that man" had ever made any inappropriate advances towards me. They spelled out what they meant so that even a young naïve lad could easily understand. I lied to my parents! I don't know why, but I lied to them! That was what was bothering me most over the last almost five decades! I had gone against my own set of morals – Moral Injury!

Since by God's grace I have become a Christian, I have now been able to seek and to find His forgiveness for lying instead of honouring my father and mother with the truth. My heavenly Father has forgiven me through His Son Jesus Christ and His Holy Spirit testifies with His written Word that all is well between me and God and God and me. He has restored my soul.

Conclusion

Lord Jesus, I trust You. You alone are my hope. You are my solace. You are my Light in that dark place. Help me to dwell always in the light, Your light. And I thank You that all wrongs will be righted upon Your return.

Me: Caring for the Carer

"You guide me with Your counsel, and afterward receive me to glory. Whom have I in heaven but You? And there is none on earth I desire besides You. My heart and my strength fail; but God is the strength of my heart and my portion forever"
Psalm 73:24-26.

Introduction & Definition
The terms "burnout" and "compassion fatigue" are somewhat self-explanatory. Both speak of an end result.

Burnout is a candle burning brightly for the length of its wick, now spluttering towards its end. Upon extinguishment the melted wax solidifies and is engulfed in the ensuing darkness.

Compassion Fatigue is an ambulance running out of fuel as it speeds on its way to the scene of a serious accident. It rolls to a stop at the side of the road and shuts off its lights and siren to save embarrassment. As is a candle with no wick left to burn, so is an ambulance with no fuel left to run: both are spent.

Competitors & Carers
Competitive workplaces fuel burnout. Those seeking promotion, those trying to climb corporate ladders, lack proper peer support because they are competing against their peers. Thus, they may crash and burn if they neglect self-care. Then there are those who are in the support industry, those who are the carers of their

competitive peers and others. These succumb to Compassion Fatigue due to taking to heart their peers' burdens and problems without offloading. It is a recipe for disaster when Carers themselves have to compete with their peers for recognition and promotion.

Though very much related, Burnout and Compassion Fatigue are not exactly the same thing, but when combined in an individual, they cause the competitive Carer to flat-line. Logically speaking, it would be better to have one or the other than having both Burnout and Compassion Fatigue at the same time. However, since logic lacks compassion, it would be far better to suffer from neither! Therefore, recognise the symptoms.

Symptoms

Humanly speaking, those with *Burnout* and/or *Compassion Fatigue* have nothing left to give. They are stressed-out to the max. Their vim, vigour and vitality, their drive, has been replaced by a hollow feeling: emptiness. Their zeal, zest and zing, their passion, has been turned into fatigue, and their flaming fire has become dying embers and burnt-out ash. Empathy has ceded to sympathy, which has finally surrendered to apathy. Pain-avoidance is now about self-preservation: Reflection becomes deflection as the hard-shelled tortoise retreats into itself. It is a turning inward.

"Now solitaire's the only game in town."[26] Loneliness. Withdrawal. Avoidance. The brave face works hard to conceal by disguise the broken spirit. "The tears of a clown when no one's around."[27] Salty-tears. Self-reflection. Self-pity. Self-loathing. Self-medication. "Running on empty."[28] Fatigue. Breathlessness. Anxiety. Tightened vocal cords. Gastric pains. Racing heart. Emotional pain. Hurt. Fear. Irritability. Smouldering anger. Crash. Reboot. Crash. Crash. "Someone help me, help me please. Is the answer up above?"[29] Help!

Triggers

Busyness. Competitiveness. Nurturing negative thoughts and attitudes. Being "happy" in misery. Viewing the glass as half empty and in need of a top-up. Stressful situations. Neglecting to care for self.

Cure

Self-care. Rest. Re-focus. Recalibrate. "Count your blessings, name them one by one."[30] Set smaller goals. Calm down and slow down. Relax. Unwind. De-stress. Appreciate what you have. Appreciate creation. Stop to smell the flowers. "Be still and know that I am God."[31] Be thankful. Be grateful. Be kind, especially to yourself. Seek professional help. LET, repeat, LET others help you!

---

[26] Neil Sedaka & Phil Cody.

[27] Hank Crosby, Smokey Robinson and Stevie Wonder.

[28] Jackson Browne.

[29] Paul Anka.

[30] Johnson Oatman.

[31] Psalm 46:10a.

Having noted earlier that "there is significant overlap between the symptoms of PTSD and moral injury",[32] the following is worth noting, where Curtis Solomon says,

> After all, many people, especially those in the first responder community, don't experience Post-Traumatic Stress symptoms until they quit, retire, or switch career fields. When faced with one emergency after another, it's common to press forward without ever processing. People tend to stay in alert mode, being constantly distracted by the next emergency. While many can live by this pattern for a while, it often catches up to them eventually. You, in fact, might notice that unprocessed trauma will gradually (or suddenly) come to the surface. I tell retiring police officers, firefighters, EMTs, and combat veterans to be on the lookout for things to start popping up as they slow down. It is helpful to prepare for change and not be caught off guard by it.[33]

Relapse Prevention Plan

You have not failed if you are burnt out. You have not let the side down if you are compassion fatigued.

---

[32] Rhiannon Neilsen, *Moral Injury: Unseen Wounds in an Age of Barbarism*, (Edited by Tom Frame), University of New South Wales Press Ltd, 2015, 136.
[33] Curtis Solomon, *I Have PTSD: Reorienting After Trauma*, New Growth Press, Greensboro, NC, 2023, 4.

You have simply neglected self-care. Self-care is not a sin. Nor is it a crime. It is just something that you must do, if you are going to fulfil your responsibilities to your job, your family, your friends and yourself. Sick and ill doctors have to cancel the appointments of the sick and ill. A helpless helper is useless. Like the oxygen masks on airplanes, therefore, look after your own wellbeing – first! It is sensible, not selfish, to look after yourself.

- Burnout and Compassion Fatigue have KO'd even champions
- Learn the symptoms to avoid the punches
- Eat well, and train your mind as well as your body before entering the ring
- Take time between each round to self-assess and have others assess your present condition
- If you are face down on the canvass, then listen closely to the count before you even think of trying to get back into the fray
- Don't forget to relax between title bouts

Conclusion & My Personal Care

Read Bible daily. Reflect on passage. Pray. Instead of always running around the lake or through the park, occasionally have a relaxing walk while enjoying and appreciating God's creation. Listen to the birdsong. Even sing along with the birds! Be thankful to God, for the sun sparkling on the water, for the breeze in the trees, for all of His handiwork.

Don't just glorify God. Enjoy Him too! Really enjoy Him! Relax on my own. Relax with my wife. Relax with my family. Relax in my spa. Relax on my couch. Relax through the night in my bed. Relax! Don't let politics annoy. Don't let busy traffic annoy. Don't let Social Media annoy. Stay calm. Stay focussed. Be grateful for family and friends.

I thought I was looking after myself. It was only after I had crashed that I realised how much I wasn't. I did not enjoy getting KO'd and "canvassed"! But God certainly got my attention while I was seeing stars!

The chief end of man is to glorify God and to <u>enjoy</u> Him forever.[34]

---

[34] Westminster Shorter Catechism Q & A 1.

God: The Declaration of Peace

"The word that Isaiah the son of Amoz saw concerning Judah and Jerusalem. Now it shall come to pass in the latter days that the mountain of the LORD's house shall be established on the top of the mountains, and shall be exalted above the hills; and all nations shall flow to it. Many people shall come and say, 'Come, and let us go up to the mountain of the LORD, to the house of the God of Jacob; He will teach us His ways, and we shall walk in His paths.' For out of Zion shall go forth the law, and the word of the LORD from Jerusalem. He shall judge between the nations, and rebuke many people; they shall beat their swords into plowshares, and their spears into pruning hooks; nation shall not lift up sword against nation, neither shall they learn war anymore. O house of Jacob, come and let us walk in the light of the LORD." Isaiah 2:1-5

Introduction

Isaiah lived some 700 years before Christ. Many call his wonderful book *The Gospel According To Isaiah* on account of him speaking so much about the Good News of the Messiah or Christ who was to come. In the passage before us Isaiah is talking about the peace that Christ and His kingdom will bring on earth. Isaiah speaks of nations beating their swords into ploughshares and their spears into pruning hooks, which is to say that the nations will stop fighting with each other, "neither shall they learn war anymore."

In some ways Remembrance Day, or Poppy Day as some refer to it, reminds us of what God through His Prophet Isaiah is speaking of. For Remembrance Day, or Armistice Day as it used to be called, recalls to our mind a time when peace was declared.

Remembrance Day began as a memorial celebrating the signing of the armistice at the 11th hour of the 11th day of the 11th month in 1918. From there it developed into celebrating the actual end of WWI, The Great War, on 28th June 1919. The main point of it all being that on Remembrance Day those who died in the line of duty while defending us as a people are remembered.

The remembrance poppy came about because of the poem written about the First World War called "In Flanders Fields." The red poppies that grew on the battlefields came to symbolise the blood that was shed defending our freedom.

War is hell. There is no glamour to it. Yes, stories of bravery, courage and heroism are legion, but primarily these are simply acts of desperate people doing desperate things in desperate times. We honour all who fought and all who died defending our Western freedoms, and hopefully as we get into our text we will see something of the positive influence that the Word of God has had on the nations including ours.

Tom Frame alerts us to the shift of thinking that started taking place in the West at the conclusion of WWI,

> The description of the Great War as the 'war to end all wars' was a theological conclusion that war could no longer be fought by moral means for just ends. Armed conflict was too ambiguous. By 1939, a seismic shift in thinking was complete in Western theology: war was no longer a moral crusade but a tragic necessity. But the same theological themes could be applied – the Good Samaritan story taught that the capacity to help created a duty to do so, and the plight of nations subjugated by totalitarianism demanded a response.[35]

In the following we'll look at a couple of points that I wish to bring to your notice from our text. Like the old hymn with the words, "Onward Christian soldiers, marching as to war, with the cross of Jesus going on before", we'll try to keep a military metaphor going…

Marching In

Notice what Isaiah says at the end of verse two of chapter two, "And all nations shall flow *to* it." Flow to what? "The mountain of the LORD's house." So the picture is that of nations coming to meet with God in His house.

---

[35] Tom Frame, *Moral Injury: Unseen Wounds in an Age of Barbarism*, (Edited by Tom Frame), University of New South Wales Press Ltd, 2015, 239.

Napoleon Bonaparte said, "An army marches on its stomach." That may conjure up a strange picture in your mind of people in uniforms crawling on their bellies, but Napoleon simply meant that armies have to be fed to be of any use. And so it is with us as Christians. Therefore, I need to feed us a bit of background knowledge to help us to understand what we're looking at:

You'll remember that at the time of Moses God had His people erect a tabernacle according to His instructions. God designed it even down to the furniture it was to be fitted with, tables and tongs, lights and lampstands, and even the Ark of the Covenant that was to be deposited therein. This tabernacle was called "The Tent of Meeting" (Exodus 40:2). God, as represented by a cloud, would descend and fill the tent with His glory. The people of God would march up and camp all around the tent but only Moses got to go in and meet with the Commander, i.e., the Captain of the LORD's Army, in this "Tent of Meeting."

In the course of time the Tabernacle was replaced by a stone Temple on a mountain in Jerusalem at the time of Solomon. Just as there was in the Tabernacle or "Tent of Meeting" so there was a room in the Temple called "the Holy of Holies," and it was in this room the God had them place the Ark of the Covenant which represented the presence of God. Only the High Priest got to go in there once a year on the Day of Atonement. He went in to pour the blood of sacrifice on the Seat of Atonement or the Mercy Seat which was the lid of the Ark that contained the stone tablets with the Ten Commandments written on them.

Now, so that we understand what's going on in our text it's important to know that The Day of Atonement was a sort of Remembrance Day ceremony. Only there was no laying of a wreath or a placing of a red poppy but rather there was a sprinkling of blood on the Mercy Seat. This was to remind the people of God that they needed to have their sins covered by blood, i.e., they needed to be forgiven for their sins against God.

Why? Why would human beings need to have their sins forgiven? The Bible says that there is no remission without the shedding of blood. Jesus in the Lord's Supper says, "Do this in remembrance of Me." What are we remembering in the Lord's Supper? That Christ shed His blood to cover the sins of all who believe.

Right, it is very important that we understand the broader context of what Isaiah means when he speaks of all nations marching into, or as he puts it, flowing into the LORD's house "on the top of the mountains … exalted above the hills." It means that the forgiveness of sin is for all people and not just the Jews. Isaiah is painting for us a picture of God inviting all the nations, all humanity, to come to Him to have their sins covered by Christ's shed blood and thereby be reconciled to Him.

So, the Tabernacle and then the Temple on the mount at Jerusalem were just places where people could come to meet with God and have their sins symbolically covered by blood. But again we ask the question, why? What has humanity done that we as part of all the nations should need our sins covered by blood? For "without the shedding of blood there is no remission." Hebrews 9:22b. Well, it's all because of war, i.e., the war between the human race and God. That's where all wars come from, wars as individual against individual, family against family, clan against clan, and nation against nation. These all come from our war against God! That war was started by our forefather Adam.

A little more back-briefing will help to better understand the magnitude of the good news of what Isaiah is speaking of here. If we had an easel with a map on it overlaid with transparencies, I'd have a pointer and I'd be pointing you to a geographical location on a map: The Garden of Eden!

God created Adam and put him in a beautiful garden, the Garden of Eden. Then God entered into an agreement with Adam, a covenant; that should Adam remain obedient to God for an undefined length of time, then God would bless him with even more than He had already blessed him, which is also to say that the Triune God would bless him as the head and representative of the human race, which human race of course is comprised of all the nations.

Adam knew right from wrong because God, as He has with every human being since, had written His Law on humanity's heart. Adam was to love God and his neighbour as himself. God gave Adam a wife made from one of his own ribs, and He gave what we call *The Cultural Mandate*. Adam and Eve and their future offspring were to "be fruitful and multiply; [and] fill the earth and subdue it" Genesis 1:28a. But what did Adam do? He sided with the devil and instead declared war on God. Adam as it were beat his ploughshare into a sword and his pruning hook into a spear to be used in humanity's war against God!

So, after all of that, what we have here in this beautiful piece of Scripture are words that speak of a reversal of humanity's rebellion against God. It speaks of reconciliation, "And all the nations shall flow to it," i.e., to the LORD's house which "shall be established on the top of the mountains." The nations, including you and me, will as it were march in to meet with God.

So, we are left with a couple of connected questions that we need to attempt to answer in our second point: 1. What is meant by the words there at the beginning of verse two, "Now it shall come to pass in the latter days…"? And. 2. What is meant by "The mountain of the LORD's house"? Well, to answer our second question first: There is no more Tabernacle and there is no more Temple on the mount. Therefore, either the temple will need to be rebuilt or there is something else going on in these "latter days."

Marching Out

Some 700 years after Isaiah, Jesus predicted the demolition of the Temple on the Mount which took place in 70AD. The "Wailing Wall" is the contemporary reminder of that destruction. The invading Roman armies levelled the place and many Jews who did not heed our Lord's warning to flee Jerusalem were put to the sword.

Now, as you know, there was a period of transition from Old Testament practices to New Testament practices. The Book of Acts in particular records that period of history. Practices such as Old Testament Circumcision and Passover were superseded by Jesus's introduction of New Testament Baptism and the Lord's Supper respectively.

Israel ceased to be a theocratic nation with the Roman army's demolition of the Temple as the Church as we know it began to emerge. Therefore, the LORD's house is no longer the Temple on the Mount at Jerusalem. Rather it is wherever two or three gather in Jesus's name, such as we do each Sunday as the Church. It's as Matthew Henry says about our text, "Christianity shall then be the mountain of the Lord's house. The Gospel church shall then be the rendezvous of all the spiritual seed of Abraham."

So, generally speaking the "latter days" that Isaiah is referring to is from the time of Christ, i.e., the time when the Mosaic administration was ending and the new administration of the covenant was beginning. In particular the demolition of the Temple at Jerusalem signalled the beginning of the "latter days." In other words, it was from that time that the Gospel, i.e., the Good News was sent out into *all* the nations. It is as Jesus said to His Apostles in Matthew 28:19-20, "Go therefore and make disciples of all the nations, baptising them in the name of the Father and of the Son and of the Holy Spirit, teaching them to observe all things that I have commanded you."

Again Matthew Henry looking at these verses said this, "In the last days of the earthly Jerusalem, just before the destruction of it, this heavenly Jerusalem shall be erected, Hebrews 12:22; Galatians 4:26."

In the Galatians 4:26 verse the Apostle Paul while contrasting the earthly Jerusalem which is in bondage with her children says, "but the Jerusalem above is free, which is the mother of us all." In other words, no longer is God centred at the Holy of Holies at the Temple on Temple Mount. He is now marching out of Jerusalem with His people who are filled with the Holy Spirit, the third Person of the Trinity. And the message His people are to proclaim as they march into all the nations is the Gospel. The Good News then truly is "The Declaration of Peace"!

So, are you beginning to understand what's going on in our text? We come to God for instruction and then God sends us out again. It's like in the Military where we attend a meeting to receive our orders then we go out from the meeting to put those orders into practice.

When I was becoming an army chaplain my eldest brother said, "Great! God's army is invading the Australian army!" We Christians belong to God's army. The difference between God's Army and the Australian Army is that we already have beaten our swords into ploughshares and our spears into pruning hooks. Our banner is Christ and His cross, the banner of peace! Again, as the old hymn puts it, "Onward Christian soldiers, marching as to war, with the cross of Jesus going on before."

For part of my training when I was becoming an army chaplain was to be sent to the Royal Military College at Duntroon, (RMC) to learn how to be an officer. Early each morning we formed up on the parade ground and were marched up to the top of the hill and fed breakfast and then we were marched back down again. It was kind of like the Grand Old Duke of York, "He marched us up to the top of the hill, and then he marched us down again!"

They give you breakfast in the mess at the top of the hill, and it's all-you-can eat. I stuffed my face on the first morning only to discover when they marched us down again that we had to do Physical Training (PT) for a whole hour. It was a real battle to hold my breakfast down. I learned my lesson. Next morning I only had a small bowl of healthy cereal!

What our text is teaching us is that God's people come together to meet with Him to be fed by Him. We are marched up to the top of the hill! Then after we are fed, we go out and put into practice whatever we have been taught. And, unlike eating physical food before doing physical labour, we are able to stomach swallowing spiritual food before performing spiritual labour! In Old Testament times God's people at least four times a year for annual feasts would walk up the hill to the Temple and then they would walk back down again.

Nowadays we gather together at church every Sunday where we are taught from Scripture and then we disperse again out into the community hopefully after having a "mountaintop experience". Another way of looking at this, if you will, is that of the living and true God breathing in and then breathing out. His breath draws us in and then He sends us out again full of His Word and His Spirit on the first day of every seven. Thus, He marches us up to the top of the hill and He marches us down again.

What does God do with us at the top of the hill, i.e., in church of a Sunday? Well, we see there in verse three that, "He will teach us His ways, and we shall walk in His paths." His ways are good ways, and His paths are well-lit paths.

One of the chaplains I was training with badly sprained his ankle. We were out doing some night navigation with luminous compasses among the gum trees under a million stars when he put his foot in a hole. He was on crutches for the rest of our time down there! God's paths of righteousness may be narrow but, unlike the ways of the world, they are bright with no potholes lurking in the creepy shadows.

And look what it says at the end of verse three, "For out of Zion shall go forth the law, and the word of the LORD from Jerusalem." Just before He went up to heaven from whence He came, Jesus told His disciples to "tarry in Jerusalem" where they would receive the "Promise of the Father." i.e., the Holy Spirit who is also known as the Breath of God.

His followers were to gather in Jerusalem where they would meet with God the Holy Spirit and then they were to take God's Word, the Gospel of Peace, into all the nations. They were to "Go therefore and make disciples of all the nations, baptising [and] teaching them." And so God's Law and Gospel began to spread throughout the world even to this very day. God's Law shows us our need for Christ and God's Gospel shows us how He saves us.

Like love and marriage going together like a horse and carriage, when it comes to Law and Gospel, you can't have one without the other. The Gospel saves us from the Law's condemnation. You know that you have been saved and are no longer under the condemnation of God's Law when you begin to beat your sword into a ploughshare and your spear into a pruning hook. This is to return from the battlefield to the Garden as it were.

And notice what Isaiah through the Holy Spirit is saying about whole nations. "Nation shall not lift up sword against nation, neither shall they learn war anymore." Isaiah 2:4b. Yes, but what about all the wars of recent history? The Napoleonic Wars, the Boer War, the Crimean War, the First World War, the Second World War and so forth? Well, this alerts us to the idea that maybe the time of world peace is not quite yet but rather is up ahead.

Of course, most if not all of the Western nations have been Christianised to various extents. One only has to look at the debates that armies of Militant Atheism are having on social media and even public media to see the influence Christianity has had on society. The recent debate over the definition of marriage attests to it! Should we retain the Biblical definition rather than change it to the Secular definition? That is the question.

So, we see that the time of national peace with God has not quite yet arrived. Therefore, could it be that there is a future Golden Age ahead, a period when the world is at peace with itself and with God? Well, here we are in the nation of Australia hearing about God's Declaration of Peace! Are they hearing God's declaration of peace in any other nations? New Zealand? Canada? America? Scotland? England?

It's happening, isn't it? The Good News is spreading. The leaven is leavening the whole batch. The mustard seed is slowly growing into a giant tree! To be sure Christ's Kingdom is not *of* this world. It is an invisible entity. It is spiritual. But it certainly is *in* this world and the influence and growth of Christ's

Kingdom cannot be denied. It started in Jerusalem. "For out of Zion shall go forth the law, and the word of the LORD from Jerusalem." Isaiah 2:3b.

Would you agree with me that Christianity is still spreading among the nations? That it's no longer contained in Jerusalem but is marching out into all the world? I hear the Gospel is making huge inroads in China, India and South America.

Anyway, enough prayers have gone up over the centuries seeking for God to bring this about. The so called Lord's Prayer, "Our Father which art in heaven, hallowed be Thy name, Thy kingdom come, Thy will be done on earth as it is in heaven..." Those are the words Jesus taught His disciples to pray, those are the words that God's Army are praying. Therefore, it is the promise of God that there will be a time of world peace, for God cannot break His Word!

Conclusion

As we conclude, remember then where Remembrance Day fits into the grand scheme of things. It's a hint of things to come. And remember where you fit in. You are part of God's Army and you have the message of peace, The Declaration of Peace, whether it's through telling others about Christ or simply inviting them to church so that they will hear the Gospel. Therefore, don't be "forsaking the assembling of ourselves together, as is the manner of some, but exhorting one another, and so much the more as you see the Day approaching" Hebrews 10:25.

And be encouraged, the promise of God still stands: "Nation shall not lift up sword against nation, neither shall they learn war anymore."